SLITHERING SNAKE

a picture book and song

written & illustrated by

Steph Plant

Printed in the United States of America

ISBN-13: 978-0692990865 (Steph Plant)
ISBN-10: 0692990860

First Printing, 2017

Stephanie R. Plant
www.stephplantbooks.com

To all my friends and
family who supported
me in this process,
especially Micah.

slithering

slithering

slithering

snake

lives on the land

or lives in a lake

he doesn't have arms

and he doesn't have legs

when he
was young

he popped
out of an egg

slithering

slithering

slithering

snake

slithering

slithering

slithering

snake

tree snake

python

anaconda

viper

garter

black mamba

diamondback

copperhead

big boa

coral snake

corn snake

king cobra

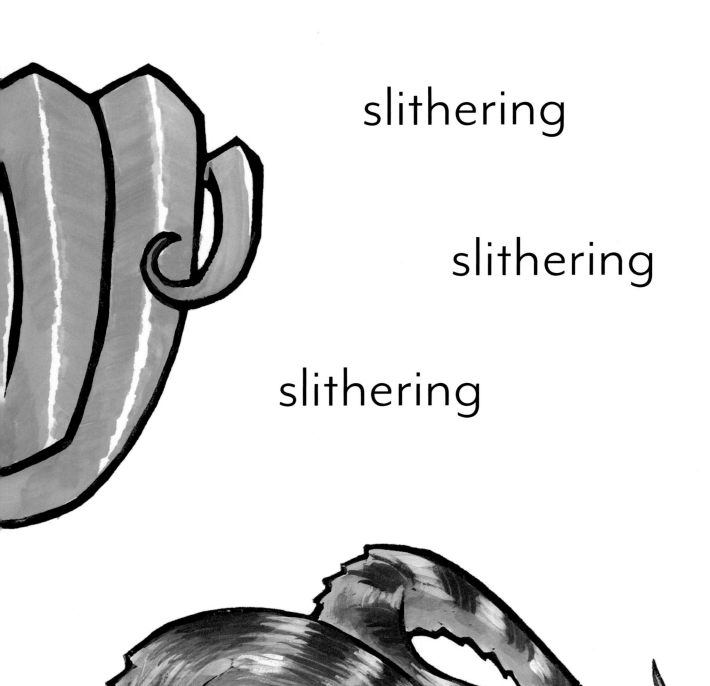

slithering

slithering

slithering

snake

lives on the land

or lives in a lake

he's very afraid

so he slithers away

slithering

slithering

slithering

snake

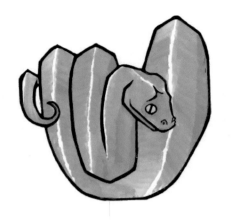

Green Tree Python

-non-venomous constrictor

-lives in trees in the rainforests around Australia and Indonesia

-they eat rodents and reptiles and lure their prey by wiggling the tip of their tails

Ball Python

- non-venomous constrictor

-lives in the flatlands of Sub-Saharan Africa

-they eat small mammals and rodents

-they coil into a tight ball when approached by a predator

Anaconda

-non-venomous constrictor

-lives in the wetlands of South America

-they eat amphibians, birds, and fish

-this species gives birth to live young

Desert Horned Viper

-venomous snake

-lives in the deserts of the Arabian Peninsula

-they eat rodents, birds, and lizards

-the horned viper buries itself in the sand to hide

Common Garter Snake

-harmless snake

-lives throughout North America

-they eat worms, lizards, frogs, rodents, and eggs

-some birds of prey make a meal out of garter snakes

Black Mamba

-venomous snake

-lives in the woods and rocky parts of
 sub-Saharan Africa

-they eat small mammals and birds

-mambas are one of the fastest snakes

Diamondback Rattlesnake

-venomous snake

-lives in dry, rocky areas in southwestern USA and northern Mexico

-they eat rodents and other small mammals

-these snakes rattle their tails when they are approached by a predator

Copperhead

-venomous snake

-lives in central, southern, and eastern USA and northern Mexico

-they eat rodents, frogs, and insects

-very good at camouflage

Boa Constrictor

-non-venomous constrictor

-lives in tropical areas of North, Central, and South America

-they eat mammals and birds

-nocturnal snake

Coral Snake

-venomous snake

-lives southern USA and northern Mexico

-they eat smaller snakes, reptiles, birds, and small rodents

-their fangs are not retractable

Corn Snake

-non-venomous constrictor

-lives in central and southeastern USA and northern Mexico

-they eat mostly rodents

-also known as the rat snake

King Cobra

-venomous snake

-lives in forested areas of southern China, India and Southeast Asia

-they eat small mammals, lizards, and eggs

-they have excellent vision

"Slithering Snake"

scan the image below on your smartphone to direct you to the audio download website
(www.stephplantmusic.bandcamp.com/track/slithering-snake)

written by Steph Plant

recorded and mixed by Adam Long

vocals & guitar : Steph Plant

piano & percussion : Sarah Vie

My Relief Block Printmaking Technique

1.

Use sharp tools to carve the image out of a piece of linoleum.

2.

Roll ink on the carved block and place a piece of paper on the wet ink. Rub the paper to imprint the reverse image from the block to the paper.

3.

Use watercolor paint to fill in the images with color.

Made in the USA
Lexington, KY
17 December 2017